Feelings
ALPHABET

FITCHBURG PUBLIC SCHOOLS
EARLY CHILDHOOD PROGRAMS
COMMUNITY PARTNERSHIPS/ 188

Feelings
ALPHABET
An Album of Emotions from A to Z

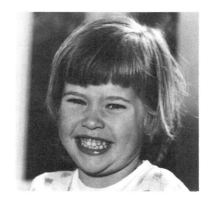

Judy Lalli, M.S.

ᒣ

JALMAR PRESS
Rolling Hills Estates, California

Copyright © 1984 by Judith M. Lalli
All Rights Reserved

Published by Jalmar Press
45 Hitching Post Drive, Building 2
Rolling Hills Estates, California 90274

**Previously published by B.L. Winch & Associates
under same title, first edition 1988.**

No part of this book may be reproduced by any mechanical,
photographic, or electronic process, or in the form of a
photographic recording, nor may it be stored in a retrieval
system, transmitted or otherwise copied for public or private use
without the written permission of the publisher.

Production Coordinator: Janet Lovelady
Photography: Douglas L. Mason-Fry
Graphics: Nancy Snyder

Special thanks to: Harry Brown and Linda Nyce-Landis

Printing No.   10 9 8 7 6 5 4 3 2 1

Library of Congress Cataloging in Publication Data

Lalli, Judy. 1949-
    Feelings alphabet.

    Summary: Each letter of the alphabet is represented by a
captioned photograph illustrating a different feeling or emotion.
    1. Emotions—Juvenile literature.   2. Alphabet—Juvenile literature
[1. Alphabet.   2. Emotions]
I. Title.
BF561.L35   1984   372.4'145   83-51343

ISBN 0-915190-82-6 (pbk.)

For Tony

INTRODUCTION

I created FEELINGS ALPHABET out of my conviction that the children who are able to acknowledge and express their feelings will be the ones who will be able to learn. When we succeed at learning, we feel good about ourselves. At the same time, we can't learn *unless* we feel good about ourselves. Hence, FEELINGS ALPHABET is an *enabling* book.

FEELINGS ALPHABET is also an ABC book, designed to teach alphabet letters to young children. Beginning readers will learn to read and comprehend the words depicted on each page. But, more importantly, FEELINGS ALPHABET is a tool for teaching children about themselves. Familiar feelings are captured in delightful, ''one-of-a-kind'' photographs and their meanings are highlighted with individualized lettering. Naming each feeling fosters an awareness that emotions are universal, they are special, *and* they matter. Exploring an alphabet of feelings with a child reinforces this important lesson: feelings in themselves are not good or bad — they just are.

Children instantly identify with the kids in FEELINGS ALPHABET:

> ''I like the boy who is frustrated. When I don't get my way, sometimes I cry and slam my door.''

> ''The silly picture shows what I like to do. I like to make my baby sister giggle.''

As they recognize and share experiences of embarrassment, pride, or disappointment, younger readers will enlarge their knowledge of human nature and develop greater tolerance of others.

Children will gain a sense of accomplishment as they learn to read these feelings words and relate to the ideas. They will find joy as they become adept at expressing themselves more fully. Self-awareness and self-acceptance will grow, page by page.

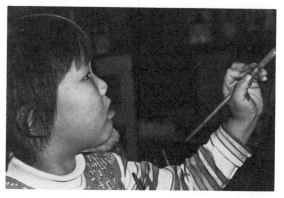

How do you feel today?

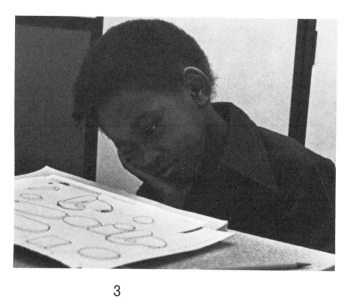

afraid

BRAVE

Curious?

Disappointed

~~Fustatid~~

~~Frustated~~

~~Frastratid~~

~~Frustrited~~

Frustrated!

giggly

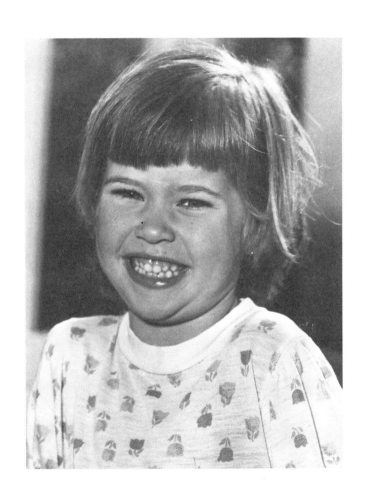

Helpful

INVOLVED

JOYFUL!

kissable

Loving

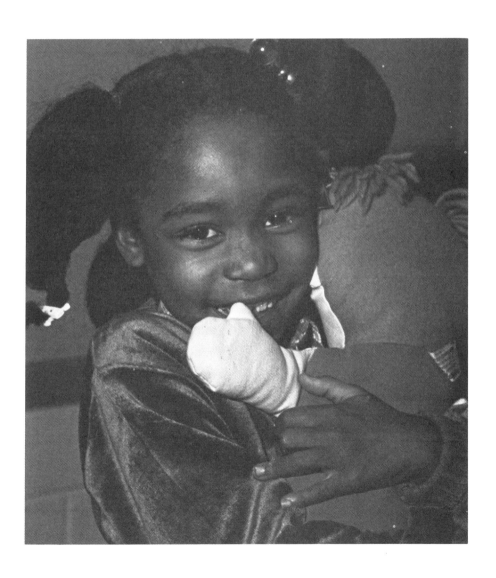

MISERABLE

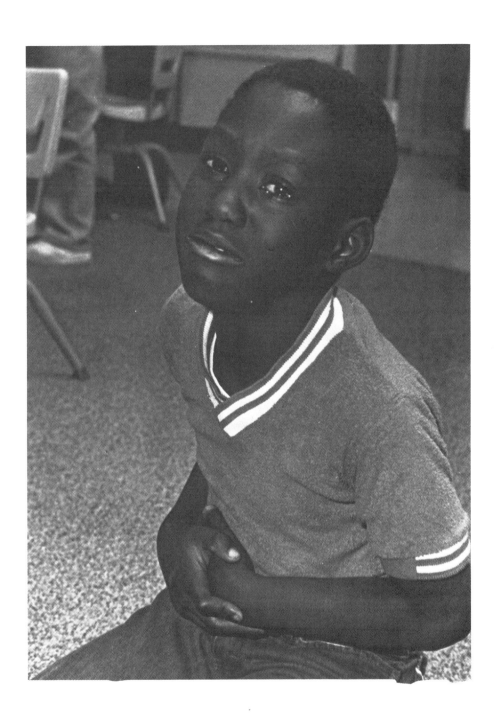

Nervous

O.K.

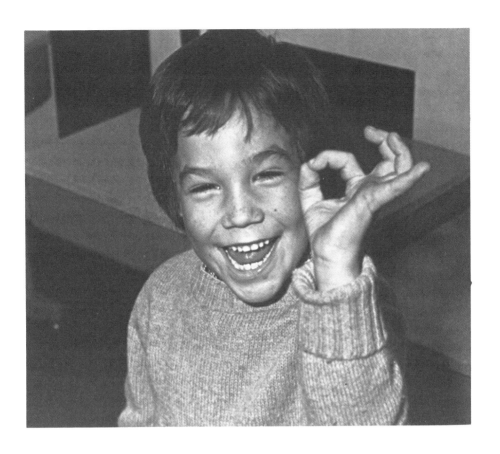

PROUD

Quiet

relaxed

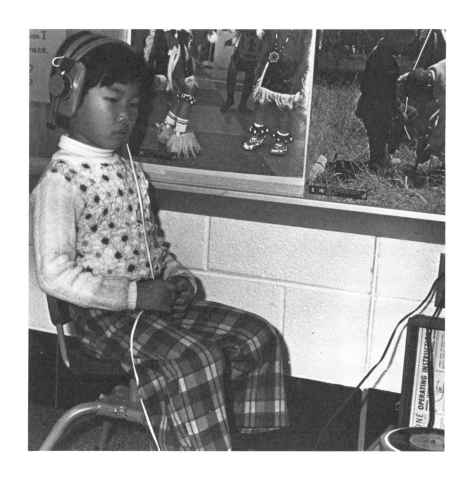

Silly

VAIN

wishy-washy

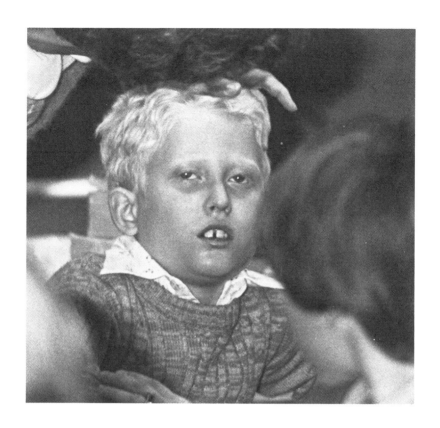

56

The end

ABOUT THE AUTHOR

JUDY LALLI, M.S., a first-grade teacher in Norristown, Pennsylvania, has been teaching for twelve years. She holds B.S. and M.S. degrees in elementary education from the University of Pennsylvania, and she has completed extensive postgraduate work in the fields of reading instruction and human development. Her background in these areas led her to write her first book, *At Least I'm Getting Better* (Impact, 1981), a delightful blend of poems and photographs dealing with children's feelings and relationships. *Feelings Alphabet* also grew out of her work with emotions and self-concept in children.

Judy Lalli has directed and performed in many local and dinner theater productions. She loves her family, the color purple, walking on the beach, talking on the phone, and making her friends laugh. She describes herself as "...compulsive about some things, absent-minded about others, very emotional — and always, always ready to celebrate life!"

ABOUT THE PHOTOGRAPHER

DOUGLAS L. MASON-FRY has taught industrial arts for ten years. He has been taking pictures for much longer than that. Currently, he does wedding and fine art photography in Lancaster, Pennsylvania. *Feelings Alphabet* is Doug's second collaboration with Judy Lalli: his charming and sensitive photographs appear in *At Least I'm Getting Better.*

ABOUT THE GRAPHIC ARTIST

NANCY SNYDER is an illustrator and designer living in Norristown, Pennsylvania. She holds a Bachelor of Fine Arts degree in illustration from Moore College of Art, where she currently teaches part-time. In addition to her freelance work, Nancy does courtroom art for WCAU-TV in Philadelphia.

. WINCH & ASSOCIATES
LMAR PRESS

Creative Teaching Series

Learning The Skills of Peacemaking
An Activity Guide for Elementary-Age Children

"Global peace begins with you. Guide develops this fundamental concept in fifty lessons. If this curriculum was a required course in every elementary school in every country, we would see world peace in our children's lifetimes." — *Letty Cottin Pogrebin*, Ms. Magazine
0-915190-46-X $21.95
8½ × 11 paperback, illus.

Project Self-Esteem EXPANDED
A Parent Involvement Program for Elementary-Age Children

An innovative parent-support program that promotes children's self-worth. "Project Self Esteem is the most extensively tested and affordable drug and alcohol preventative program available."

0-915190-59-1 $39.95
8½ × 11 paperback, illus.

The Two Minute Lover
Announcing A New Idea In Loving Relationships

No one is foolish enough to imagine that s/he *automatically* deserves success. Yet, almost everyone thinks that they automatically deserve sudden and continuous success in marriage. Here's a book that helps make that belief a reality.
0-915190-52-4 $9.95
6 × 9 paperback, illus.

Reading, Writing and Rage
An autopsy of one profound school failure, disclosing the complex processes behind it and the secret rage that grew out of it.

Must reading for anyone working with learning disabled, functional illiterates, or juvenile delinquents.

0-915190-42-7 $16.95
5½ × 8½ paperback

Feel Better Now
30 Ways to Handle Frustration in Three Minutes or Less

Most of us realize that letting go of tension is a key to happiness and health. This book explains the dynamics of letting go.

0-915190-66-4 $9.95
6 X 9 paperback

Esteem Builders
You CAN improve your students' behavior and achievement through building self-esteem. Here is a book packed with classroom- proven techniques, activities, and ideas you can immediately use in your own program or at home.

Ideas, ideas, ideas, for grades K-8 and parents.
0-915190-53-2 $39.95
8½ × 11 paperback, illus.

Good Morning Class—I Love You!
Thoughts and Questions About Teaching from the Heart

A book that helps create the possibility of having schools be places where students, teachers and principals get what every human being wants and needs—LOVE!

0-915190-58-3 $6.95
5½ × 8½ paperback, illus.

I am a blade of grass
A Breakthrough in Learning and Self-Esteem

Help your students become "lifetime learners," empowered with the confidence to make a positive difference in their world (without abandoning discipline or sacrificing essential skill and content acquisition).
0-915190-54-0 $14.95
6 × 9   paperback, illus.

Unlocking Doors to Self-Esteem
Presents innovative ideas to make the secondary classroom a more positive learning experience—socially and emotionally—for students and teachers. Over 100 lesson plans included. Designed for easy infusion into curriculum. Gr. 7-12

0-915190-60-5 $16.95
6 × 9 paperback, illus

SAGE: *Self-Awareness Growth Experiences*

A veritable treasure trove of activities and strategies promoting positive behavior and meeting the personal/social needs of young people in grades 7-12. Organized around affective learning goals and objectives. Over 150 activities.
0-915190-61-3   **$16.95**
6 × 9 paperback, illus.

**B.L. WINCH & ASSOCIATES
JALMAR PRESS**

Creative Parenting Series

Pajamas Don't Matter:
(or What Your Baby Really Needs)

Here's help for new parents everywhere! Provides valuable information and needed reassurances to new parents as they struggle through the frantic, but rewarding, first years of their child's life.
0-915190-21-4 $5.95
8½ × 11 paperback, full color

Why Does Santa Celebrate Christmas?

What do wisemen, shepherds and angels have to do with Santa, reindeer and elves? Explore this Christmas fantasy which ties all of the traditions of Christmas into one lovely poem for children of all ages.
0-915190-67-2 $12.95
8 1/2 x 11 hardcover, full color

Feelings Alphabet

Brand-new kind of alphabet book full of photos and word graphics that will delight readers of all ages."...lively, candid...the 26 words of this pleasant book express experiences common to all children." *Library Journal*
0-935266-15-1 $7.95
6 × 9 paperback, B/W photos

The Parent Book

A functional and sensitive guide for parents who want to enjoy every minute of their child's growing years. Shows how to live with children in ways that encourage healthy emotional development. Ages 3-14.
0-915190-15-X $9.95
8½ × 11 paperback, illus.

Aliens In My Nest
SQUIB Meets The Teen Creature

Squib comes home from summer camp to find that his older brother, Andrew, has turned into a snarly, surly, defiant, and non-communicative adolescent. *Aliens* explores the effect of Andrew's new behavior on Squib and the entire family unit.
0-915190-49-4 $7.95
8½ × 11 paperback, illus.

Hugs & Shrugs
The Continuing Saga of SQUIB

Squib feels incomplete. He has lost a piece of himself. He searches everywhere only to discover that his missing piece has fallen in and not out. He becomes complete again once he discovers his own inner-peace.

0-915190-47-8 $7.95
8½ × 11 paperback, illus.

**Moths & Mothers/
Feather & Fathers**
A Story About a Tiny Owl Named SQUIB

Squib is a tiny owl who cannot fly. Neither can he understand his feelings. He must face the frustration, grief, fear, guilt and loneliness that we all must face at different times in our lives. Struggling with these feelings, he searches, at least, for understanding.

0-915190-57-5 $7.95
8½ × 11 paperback, illus.

Hoots & Toots & Hairy Brutes
The Continuing Adventures of SQUIB

Squib—who can only toot—sets out to learn how to give a mighty hoot. His attempts result in abject failure. Every reader who has struggled with life's limitations will recognize their own struggles and triumphs in the microcosm of Squib's forest world. A parable for all ages from 8 to 80.

0-915190-56-7 $7.95
8½ × 11 paperback, illus.

Do I Have To Go To School Today?
Squib Measures Up!

Squib dreads the daily task of going to school. In this volume, he daydreams about all the reasons he has not to go. But, in the end, Squib convinces himself to go to school because his teacher accepts him "Just as he is!"

0-915190-62-1 $7.95
8½ × 11 paperback, illus.

The Turbulent Teens
Understanding Helping Surviving

"This book should be read by every parent of a teenager in America...It gives a parent the information needed to understand teenagers and guide them wisely."—Dr. Fitzhugh Dodson, author of *How to Parent, How to Father*, and *How to Discipline with Love*.
0-913091-01-4 $8.95
6 × 9 paperback.

B.L. WINCH & ASSOCIATES / JALMAR PRESS

Right Brain/Whole Brain Learning Series

Openmind/Wholemind
Parenting & Teaching Tomorrow's Children Today

A book of powerful possibilities that honors the capacities, capabilities, and potentials of adult and child alike. Uses Modalities, Intelligences, Styles and Creativity to explore how the brain-mind system acquires, processes and expresses experience. Foreword by M. McClaren & C. Charles.
0-915190-45-1 $14.95
7 × 9   paperback
81 B/W photos   29 illus.

Present Yourself! *Captivate Your Audience With Great Presentation Skills*

Become a presenter who is a dynamic part of the message. Learn about Transforming Fear, Knowing Your Audience, Setting The Stage, Making Them Remember and much more. Essential reading for anyone interested in the art of communication. Destined to become the standard work in its field.
0-915190-51-6   paper $9.95
0-915190-50-8   cloth $18.95
6 × 9   paper/cloth. illus.

Unicorns Are Real
A Right-Brained Approach to Learning

Over 100,000 sold. The long-awaited "right hemispheric" teaching strategies developed by popular educational specialist Barbara Vitale are now available. Hemispheric dominance screening instrument included.
0-915190-35-4 $12.95
8½ × 11   paperback, illus.

Unicorns Are Real Poster

Beautifully-illustrated. Guaranteed to capture the fancy of young and old alike. Perfect gift for unicorn lovers, right-brained thinkers and all those who know how to dream. For classroom, office or home display.

JP9027 $4.95
19 × 27   full color

Imagination is the unicorn that lifts us above the mundane chains that bind the minds of many and flies us on fantastic wings to a place where dreams DO come true.

Practical Application, Right Hemisphere Learning Methods

Audio from Barbara Vitale. Discover many practical ways to successfully teach right-brained students using whole-to-part learning, visualization activities, color stimuli, motor skill techniques and more.
JP9110 $12.95
Audio Cassette

Don't Push Me, I'm Learning as Fast as I Can

Barbara Vitale presents some remarkable insights on the physical growth stages of children and how these stages affect a child's ability, not only to learn, but to function in the classroom.
JP9112 $12.95
Audio Cassette

Metaphoric Mind (Revised Ed.)

Here is a plea for a balanced way of thinking and being in a culture that stands on the knife-edge between catastrophe and transformation. The metaphoric mind is asking again, quietly but insistently, for equilibrium. For, after all, equilibrium is the way of nature.
0-915190-68-0 $14.95
7 × 10 paperback, B/W photos

Free Flight *Celebrating Your Right Brain*

Journey with Barbara Vitale, from her uncertain childhood perceptions of being "different" to the acceptance and adult celebration of that difference. A book for right-brained people in a left-brained world. Foreword by Bob Samples.
0-915190-44-3 $9.95
5½ × 8½   paperback, illus.

"He Hit Me Back First!"
Self-Esteem through Self-Discipline

Simple techniques for guiding children toward self-correcting behavior as they become aware of choice and their own inner authority.
0-915190-36-2   **$12.95**
8½ × 11   paperback, illus.

Learning To Live, Learning To Love

An inspirational message about the importance of love in everything we do. Beautifully told through words and pictures. Ageless and timeless.
0-915190-38-9 $7.95
6 × 9   paperback, illus.

B.L. WINCH & ASSOCIATES
JALMAR PRESS

T.A. & Warm Fuzzy Series

TA For Tots
(and other prinzes)
Over 500,000 sold.

This innovative book has helped thousands of young children and their parents to better understand and relate to each other. Ages 4-9.
0-915190-12-5 $12.95
8½ × 11 paper, color, illus.

TA For Tots, Vol. II

Explores new ranges of feelings and suggests solutions to problems such as feeling hurt, sad, shy, greedy, or lonely.
Ages 4-9.
0-915190-25-7 $12.95
8½ × 11 paper, color, illus.

TA For Tots Coloring Book

Constructive, creative coloring fun! The charming *TA For Tots* characters help show kids that taking care of their feelings is OK! Ages 2-9.
0-915190-33-8 $1.95
8½ × 11 saddle stitched, illus.

TA Today I'm OK Poster

Cheerful, happy TA creatures help convey the most positive, upbeat message to be found. Perfect for brightening your room or office.
JP9002 $3.00
19 × 27 full color poster

TA for Kids
(and grown-ups too)
Over 250,000 sold.

The message of TA is presented in simple, clear terms so youngsters can apply it in their daily lives. Warm Fuzzies abound. Ages 9-13.
0-915190-09-5 $9.95
8½ × 11 paper, color, illus.

TA For Teens
(and other important people)
Over 100,000 sold.

Using the concepts of Transactional Analysis. Dr. Freed explains the ups and downs of adulthood without talking down to teens. Ages 13-18.
0-915190-03-6 $18.95
8½ × 11 paperback, illus.

Original Warm Fuzzy Tale
Learn about "Warm Fuzzies" firsthand.
Over 100,000 sold.

A classic fairytale...with adventure, fantasy, heroes, villains and a moral. Children (and adults, too) will enjoy this beautifully illustrated book.
0-915190-08-7 $7.95
6 × 9 paper, full color, illus.

Songs of The Warm Fuzzy
"All About Your Feelings"

The album includes such songs as Hitting is Harmful, Being Scared, When I'm Angry, Warm Fuzzy Song, Why Don't Parents Say What They Mean, and I'm Not Perfect (Nobody's Perfect).
JP9003R/C $12.95
Cassette

Tot Pac *(Audio-Visual Kit)*

Includes 5 filmstrips, 5 cassettes, 2 record LP album. A *Warm Fuzzy I'm OK* poster, 8 coloring posters, 10 Warm Fuzzies. 1 *TA for Tots* and 92 page *Leader's Manual*. No prior TA training necessary to use Tot Pac in the classroom! Ages 2-9.
JP9032 $150.00
Multimedia program

Kid Pac *(Audio-Visual Kit)*

Teachers, counselors, and parents of pre-teens will value this easy to use program. Each *Kid Pac* contains 13 cassettes, 13 filmstrips, 1 *TA For Kids*, and a comprehensive *Teacher's Guide*, plus 10 Warm Fuzzies. Ages 9-13.
JP9033 $195.00
Multimedia Program